W9-BSX-019

The Next Act

A Handbook for Graduating— From Arts or Life

Colleen Hughes Mallette

High C Diva Productions

The Next Act A Handbook for Graduating—From Arts or Life Copyright © 2017 by Colleen Hughes Mallette

All rights reserved. No part of this book may be reproduced or transmitted in any form or by any means without written permission from the author.

Produced & Published by High C Diva Productions
Printed in the U.S.A.

TheNextAct.Colleen@gmail.com
Cover Art and Illustrations by Jae Lin.

ISBN: 978-0-692-69507-4

~ My Invitation to You, from Colleen Hughes Mallette ~

Have you:

* ❖ Recently graduated from college with a degree in Fine Arts?
* ❖ Been out of school a few years and are seeking to gain a better grasp on your career?

Are you:

* ❖ Currently in a leadership role with those who have creative aspirations?
* ❖ Seeking some Diva-licious inspiration with a dash of fun?
* ❖ Looking for words that could spark an "aha" moment?
* ❖ Needing information about how to put your skill set into practical use?
* ❖ Interested in some step-by-step advice?

Would you:

* ❖ Like some guidance from someone who has been in your shoes?

Good news! If you answered yes to any of these, this book was written for you!

My desire is that you find yourself within the pages of this book. I invite you to find the direction and inspiration needed to accomplish becoming your greatest self!

The Waking
BY THEODORE ROETHKE

I wake to sleep, and take my waking slow.
I feel my fate in what I cannot fear.
I learn by going where I have to go.

We think by feeling. What is there to know?
I hear my being dance from ear to ear.
I wake to sleep, and take my waking slow.

Of those so close beside me, which are you?
God bless the Ground! I shall walk softly there,
And learn by going where I have to go.

Light takes the Tree; but who can tell us how?
The lowly worm climbs up a winding stair;
I wake to sleep, and take my waking slow.

Great Nature has another thing to do
To you and me; so take the lively air,
And, lovely, learn by going where to go.

This shaking keeps me steady. I should know.
What falls away is always. And is near.
I wake to sleep, and take my waking slow.
I learn by going where I have to go.

Source: *The Collected Poems of Theodore Roethke*
(Doubleday, 1961)

§ Contents §

Foreword   vii

Introduction   1

Have a Team and Choose Them Wisely   5

Practicing Your Art   11

Bypass Timidity   15

Reputation Is Everything   19

How to Survive a Tsunami   23

Your True North May Change from Time to Time   27

Let's Play a Game   33

Wellness for the Performer's Life   45

Stay Gracious Always without Expectation   53

Diva's Rockin' Resources   57

A Better Version of Yourself   61

Clarity through Inquiry Worksheets:
    Debut   65
    Applause   75
    Bravo   85
    Encore   87

Afterword   95

Engage with the Author   97

Foreward

By Katherine Catmull

The book you're holding, which is a joy to read, holds lots of practical tips—and some pretty deep bits of wisdom as well. If you're a working artist, or trying to become one, keep this book in your pocket.

I speak from experience. I'm primarily an author and stage/voice actor. But I'm also a playwright, teacher, and arts writer. I've sung backup in a band, directed, and even once designed a set (badly).

And much of what I've learned from over thirty years in the arts is distilled in this book. Here's one tip that sounds trivial but is actually hugely important:

"Word gets around. Were you on time? Did you know your part? Do you respond well to feedback? Are you consistent in performance? How do you treat the back stage crew?"

This is true beyond truth. Story: I sometimes used to help my producer/director husband with auditions by manning the lobby table. If an actor was nasty to me, I would draw a skull and crossbones on their resume. He would hear their audition, thank them, then throw the resume away. No one wants to work with jerks.

I love how Colleen puts the positive version of this: "Graciousness is *the ability to think in a larger and **more** inclusive way"*—which brings us to one of the many sentences in this book that I underlined twice:

"Be willing to constantly challenge your point of view. Assume that you cannot possibly 'know all the outcomes.' Adopt the attitude that, by standing in line for an interview or an audition, you will receive some great advantage in some way."

Many of the best things that have come to me in my work have come seemingly out of nowhere. But that "nowhere" always turned out to be offers I had accepted on a lark, sometimes years earlier; or favors I'd done for others; or projects or auditions that had seemed like failures at the time.

Most important of all, Colleen says this:

"What an audience desires from you is a kind of TRUTH that originates from that authentic self: **Your voice, your choices, your vulnerabilities** *are the very things that others want to experience."*

That is one deep, juicy truth. That's what the audience wants from you: your deepest self, your living soul, the realest you of all. That's what galvanizes and mesmerizes us. That's your greatest gift.

This book will help you give it.

~ Katherine Catmull

Katherine Catmull is the author of *Summer and Bird, The Radiant Road* (Penguin), co-authored *The Cabinet of Curiosities* (HarperCollins); multi-award-winning stage actor for three decades; voice actor in video games like Wizard 101 and DC Universe Online; produced and published playwright.

Introduction

The inspiration for this book originally came from the fact that I wanted to give something unique to my graduating students. The other day, I guesstimated that over 1,000 students have passed through my studio and classes. I began summing it all up. A packaged graduation gift did not properly convey my sentiments. Although I was teaching vocal skills, deep down, I felt equally concerned that the students should have the foundation for navigating the next phase. I am passionate about translating how one's education will flourish in the real world. I feel a certain obligation to honor the time and money it took to complete the degree.

There are some things I have done really well after my education. But, I have certainly had my share of embarrassments by over shooting the mark, misreading the audience, or investing unwisely. My penchant for risk-taking has opened some doors and given me some great adventures. It has also left me far from home with nothing but a long distance calling card!

So, yes, I would LOVE to spare anyone pain if I can. If this book gives you reassurance, a smile, or a helpful new perspective, then that would be satisfying.

1

My "thank you"—with a huge dose of love and gratitude—
go to these people:

- o My parents, Norma and Harry—thank you for taking me around the world and teaching me how to camp.

- o My angel daughter

- o My "high school bestie"

- o A few paramours and one ex-husband (you all served your time!)

- o Voice teachers

- o Professors

- o Friends, from all eras of life

- o People who have loaned me money

- o Skilled Body Workers and Wise Healers

- o Audiences

- o Conductors

- o The Campers

- o Colleagues. We speak the same language. With you, I know I am home.

- o Other sopranos—(A little competition is a good thing!)

- o Preachers and gurus

- o Comediennes

- o Mystics of the FUR variety

o Accompanists: to each of you, THANK YOU. Please forgive all of my abuse, but come on. . .who else is going to drag you to Keokuk, Iowa or Ogallala, Nebraska?

o Parents of students who paid me well

o My gracious son-in-law and his talented son

o My precious and magical granddaughter. Me thinks you have the "diva-spirit" in you. ☺

o Dave Wyatt of Wyatt Brand in Austin, who advised me it was time for this book to happen

o Friends. Many of you have let me crash on your couch, or provided a second family, or even SOAK in your bathtub!! For this I am truly grateful: you helped me feel less alone. I hope that, in some way, I enriched your life because, only through our connection, was it truly meaningful.

o Generous helpers who edited, vacuumed, and kept asking me "How's it going?"

o Coffee

o God, Spirit, Universal Love

Much thanks to you all! ~ Colleen

Let's get this show on the road!
The author with Shields-Collins Bray, principal keyboardist Fort Worth
Symphony Orchestra, May, 2014.

Have a Team, Choose Them Wisely.

Most people recognize how important it is to be supported by friends, family, and coworkers. I have been one of the lucky ones who always, for the most part, felt a great sense of community. Some of this is a result of cultural circumstance, and some is from innocent assumption. Fortunately, the nature of music ensemble work means always having a community!

The team I am referencing, in this chapter, is the team of people you need for perspective, encouragement, honesty, balance, play, and accountability.

Life! It's not for sissies. Most of us have no idea of how limited our thinking is because, hey, it's OUR thinking! We were brought up one way, around a certain social group, before we started branching out. Everyone you're going to bump into has an opinion based on a point of reference of how life has gone for them. Even more important though, is *a person's attitude about the nature of obstacles and how to respond.*

You will no doubt face challenges, especially if you are ambitious. I believe one needs a team of folks who are willing to offer their individual specialties. I can say with total candor that I am NEEDY. I have my places where I feel vulnerable and immature. I find that this is often a big part of the artistic personality. We operate on a fuel that gives so much in a public way, but it can burn us out or exhaust our spirit. My philosophy is that a lot of people do things in a big way because they are sometimes "scaring away their demons." For example, in my case I was extremely shy; being heard on stage was a great way to get over that.

Each human has something he or she does especially well and with ease. Remember your artistic side is that playful child-part of you. That is the juicy side. Walking alongside that, however, are the other parts of a child—fearfulness, a need for protection, a need for reassurance, and guidance.

Start noticing what the people around you specialize in.

Try some of these fun titles for your team members.

Ms. Big Shoulder to Cry On

Mr. I Can Change Your Flat Tires

Ms. I Speak the Truth

Mr. Stick to the Facts and Let's Find a Solution

Ms. Let's Go Eat a Carton of Ice Cream and Blow off the World Tonight

Mr. Visionary

Mrs. Big Ears for Listening Only

(And, finally, don't forget these two!!)

Ms. Anything You Do Is Fine

Mr. Now Let's Go Over Those Details Again

Start noticing what titles you might give the people in your life. Do you have a balance of all types? And more importantly—

What are their intentions????

Because at the end of the day, it is important to understand how each of them influences you.

Do they lift you up?

Take you higher?

Want you to stay small?

Make you a better person?

Make you doubt your inner voice?

Introduce new paths?

There are times that you need to remove people from the team, take a break from the team, or let the team know your direction and intent. It is also a very good idea to go a-huntin' when you are focusing on a new goal. Join a book club, or seek a therapist or spiritual advisor.

My favorite practice in times of crisis is to come up with a **Board of Directors**. Write down 5 or 6 famous folks, dead or alive, who you think have exquisite qualities.

For example, here was my celebrity board of directors at one point.

1) **Oprah Winfrey**

2) **Conan O'Brien**

3) **Marianne Williamson**

4) **Lily Tomlin**

5) **Willy Nelson** and

6) **Maya Angelou**

I imagined that there would be practical, visionary, playful, self-accepting kinds of love from this crowd. After you have established this hypothetical Board of Directors, journal your questions and think about what they might tell you in certain situations.

Then, choose another Board of Directors from people you already know in your everyday life. Call them whatever you like—mentors, gurus, helpers. I usually have three.

Always let them know you have chosen them and that you would like permission to occasionally, with respect for their time, run some questions by them. Ask them about their preferred style of communication. I can't tell you how many times someone's expertise on trends, facts, or life experience has saved me from being bludgeoned by my own "what's wrong with me?" thinking.

Ultimately, you will make your own choices, but there is strength in numbers. Why not benefit from someone who has already figured out an easier way?

Oh, and most importantly, be gracious, and say thank you—a lot.

Performing at Duplex Cabaret Theater, Manhattan.

Practicing Your Art

May I tell you a hidden secret of the ancients?

The tiniest amount of work on your technique, done in repetition, will make you an artist of precision, always gaining the slight edge.

Now, more than ever, the arts business is flooded with sophisticated performers, due to a rise in high school prep programs, artistic camps, etc. Good singers, with big voices and lots of repertoire, are almost a dime a dozen. However, something unseen and somewhat inexplicable happens when you have worked on those tedious exercises from your voice teacher. Your ability to caress a phrase or sing with really clean intonation on a descending line somehow makes audiences' hairs stand up on end.

The problem is that no one notices it until you don't do it well. When you step into an audition with the right "chops," you are accelerated forward in the director's ears; **you are taken seriously.** Eventually other factors take over, such as your type, voice, height. But having a professionally put together sound sends a clear message that you are capable and disciplined. The tongue twisters and vocal gymnastics that your voice teacher introduced to you are the stepping stones to becoming a pro. Let's put it this way. If the choice is between one 6' brunette baritone and another 6' brunette baritone, who do you think has the best chance of getting the role? It's going to be determined by their voice, how they move on stage, and their acting skills. All of which requires practice, dedication, and consistency.

What I want to impress upon you is that small amounts of time—15 minutes periodically, in an elevator or practice room, while paying attention to what you are doing with your ribs, your lips, and soft palate—will tone you and send a signal to your brain: *"He's got this. He's been paying attention. Let's send him some confidence juice."* Because once you're in front of an audience, you want to let go, get out of your head, and feel FREE.

Make an investment in you. I promise, if you practice on a quick jaunt up an elevator, most people's jaws will drop and wonder what playlist you are listening to. There's even the added bonus that someone might ask you for your autograph.

DIVA SHARE: I once was at a diner in a small west Texas town. The manager knew I was a singer, so he asked me to sing a song for the customers right then and there. I enthusiastically agreed. I performed "Over the Rainbow" (acapella). After the last note, people's mouths were gaped wide open. As I left I noticed an elderly woman and her attendant. They approached me and it was like out of a movie. She asked for my number, and within six months I was paid to give a home concert on the lawn for her community near July 4th and I was paid well and treated like a star.

You never know where opportunity will knocketh. Don't knock it. Pun intended.

How do you know there's a soprano at the door?

She can't find her key and she doesn't know where to come in!

A true Diva knows how to stretch herself.
With Mark Alexander, Fronterafest at Hyde Park Theater, Austin.

Bypass Timidity:
You Will Always Gain Something

There will always be someone with a bigger voice, more experience, more money, a better website, etc. Each of us is on a different spot in the continuum of life. Even though I am, for the most part outgoing, deep down, I have a kind of shyness. How interesting that I gravitated toward a career that makes one vulnerable in front of a lot of people. Often though, the very reward we receive can create limitations.

Artists are in this business of the arts to make relationships, to share an experience. Sometimes we are blindsided with the intense need to know we did well. We sang, played the guitar, or danced, and people clapped—they gave us love. The adoration felt really good. Often, this is where we start—we associate performing with approval. Over time, however, seeking validation from an audience starts to feel one-sided. An artist—in fact, every human—craves to feel organically loved just for being themselves.

It has been my experience that what an audience desires from you is a kind of TRUTH that originates from that authentic self:

Your voice, your choices, your vulnerabilities!

Those are the very things that others want to experience. In fact, the authenticity you express rings a note of truth in the crowd about what is authentic in them. Why do you think people feel so refreshed after a wonderful live show? There is a kind of mirroring, a kind of validation you have given your audience members, even if you made a mistake. They think, *"Gee, look at that character—she hurts, she loses, she wins. I do that, too."*

I encourage you to consider there are no missteps, even if you fail or come in second place. All attempts will serve you in some way. If your voice, height, or body type is not right for the part, there is no loss. You can't lose—even if you don't get the job! Ouch! Consider all attempts as pearls you are placing in your treasure chest of future success. Now, I always step into each situation—whether it is a party, an event, or waiting at the doctor's office—with this thought in mind,

> *"How can I be a contributor to this situation, and what will I allow myself to receive as contribution?"*

This question can open you up to a myriad of possibilities beyond the reason you are there. Someone might confirm your talent, or tell you about another audition, or have in their hands THE very music you've been looking for. I have had some gigs that weren't initially considered a dream-come-true, but the experience ended up being incredible—new faces and new depths of artistry. From these experiences, I have also learned that money is not always the only factor. If you think of yourself as a business, you will understand that investments are necessary; lessons, clothes, travel, websites etc. Often, the chance to hang out at a workshop or sing in an open mic event can be just the thing to keep you in the flow of networking.

I could write an entire chapter about having good boundaries and being paid what you are worth, but, for now, just remember that there are so many ways of being paid. Practice these ideas:

§ *Go to every audition with the assumption that there is a way to make it work.* I once auditioned for a musical, way down in South Texas, miles from my home, and didn't know how I was going to make it work financially with what they were paying. As it turned out, they put singers up in nice homes and provided lots of catered meals at rehearsals. I continued with that theater for three years and got to sing leading roles with a full orchestra in a big hall.

§ *Be willing to constantly challenge your point of view.* Assume that you cannot possibly know all the outcomes. Adopt the attitude that, by standing in line for an interview or an audition, you will receive some great advantage in some way. Your perception of right and wrong choices will change dramatically. You will be able to let go of the "Am I good enough? Do I fit in?" mentality.

Always ask yourself these questions:

§ *What else is possible?*

§ *Can it get any better than this?*

§ *What's right about this that I am not seeing?*

The world is your canvas!

What kind of brush strokes would you like to make on it?

It's yours to play with, yours to nurture,
and yours to protect.

Reputation is Everything
(Save ATTITUDE for Select Moments)

Word gets around.

Were you on time?

Did you know your part?

Do you respond well to feedback?

Are you consistent in performance?

How do you treat the back stage crew?

One thing that blew me away after several years of doing lots of challenging music performances with the Fort Worth Symphony Orchestra was what someone told me:

> *"You have always impressed the directors because you knew your music to a T in auditions."*

It never occurred to me that I could be LESS than prepared! I mean, usually, this was difficult, modern-type music—I was too terrified NOT to be ready. But, evidently, I had been more prepared than others who auditioned. I could not see my way to clearly and authentically express myself without total music preparation. I heard Sir Anthony Hopkins speak to acting students once, and when they asked him for important advice for success, he said, *"Know your lines."*

Having a reputation for dependability is worth its weight in gold. Eventually, you may be selected for a job because you are easy to work with!

On having a professional work ethic: Assume that:

> EVERYONE YOU MEET, TEACH, AUDITON FOR, OR SPEAK WITH—FROM NOW UNTIL FOREVER—YOU WILL ENCOUNTER AGAIN IN YOUR CAREER. EVERY GREETER AT AN AUDITION, THE SECRETARY YOU SPEAK WITH OVER THE PHONE, THE DOORMAN AT YOUR CONDO, ASSUME THAT THEY WILL REAPPEAR IN YOUR LIFE.

They will. Think of them as your future audience or casting directors. Our world is bereft of kindness. Let your unique spark be that unforgettable quality in someone's day.

On Attitude:

On this matter I will be brief. I prefer diplomacy—it's easier on the nerves. However, a well-placed hissy fit—when called for—has served me well. You have to know and be very clear of your boundaries and your value. If you have the inner feeling that time has been wasted or space violated, sometimes you have to raise your voice enough to be heard. Everyone is distracted. I wish it wasn't that way.

When the glorious soprano Beverly Sills sang for the Fort Worth Opera, she was called extremely early to have a wig and make-up sitting. She was not pleased. At one point during the sitting, she said very clearly, "I am not here for my health."

The demands on a singer's voice and psyche, especially for a lead operatic role, are expensive. Most of the time, you are the only one that is going to watch out for you. Your job is to deliver all performances in good voice—know what it takes for you to thrive! This is part of your protecting your reputation. You have an obligation to fulfill your contract. Never apologize for choices that contribute to a long-term career.

Elspeth Rae Smith from Sweetwater auditions for the MET with
"Glitter and be Gay" and a baton of course! Boston NATS.

How to Survive a Tsunami

"This shaking keeps me steady. I should know."
The Waking, Theodore Roethke

A graduating student once opened up to me about what he called his "Emotional Tsunami." I could see that he was right on the edge. My student explained how simultaneously his finances, his parents, and job offers were all up in the air, and meanwhile, he was currently in production for a show. This landslide sounded all too familiar to me.

Okay, here's what the American Red Cross instructs:

- If you hear an official tsunami warning or detect signs of a tsunami, evacuate at once.

- Take your emergency preparedness kit. Having supplies will make you more comfortable during the evacuation.

- Take your pets with you. If it is not safe for you to stay, it's not safe for them.

- Get to higher ground as far inland as possible.

Here is my interpretation of this information:

Pay attention and breathe. Keep your beloved friends and advisors close at hand. Keep some food and supplies handy just in case. And take time to pray, meditate, or sit by a tree to see things from a higher perspective.

A wonderful healer reminded me, "It's always sunnier on top of a cloud."

Here are some **DIVA THOUGHTS** that can help you when on shaky ground:

1. Try to look at this as a temporary period (six weeks, three months). Going back to the example of my student, part of his problem was that his parents wanted answers from him about how he was going to earn money while he still didn't have many details nailed down and had not even taken his final exams. I advised him to consider only small chunks of time and figure out how to navigate that period, instead of trying to figure out an entire year. This timing would buy him the precious time needed to make more thoughtful decisions after finals were over. Many people don't realize being in a production during school is like have a part time job. It's all-consuming. Breathe deep. Seriously. Take your day, your week, in tiny bite-size chunks

and give yourself credit for every positive step forward. How do you eat an elephant? One. Bite. At. A. Time.

2. Tsunamis are powerful and life altering, BUT they do come and go. Try making one or two small choices per day that will give you a greater sense of power or control. It could be more sleep or taking time for quiet meditation or short walks. One of my favorite sayings goes, "When things feel out of control, control what you can." It's about clicking our rhythms back into shape via SLEEP, FOOD, MOVEMENT, etc. A wonderful writer told me after she experienced a head injury, she gave herself permission to take a pleasant walk three times per day, instead of taking an antidepressant. WOW.

3. Sometimes the tsunami is not all about you—it might be more about your environment—but it IS still a tsunami. So, you need to do what you can to get out of there quickly and alive.

4. Finally, when it's over: CONGRATULATE AND THANK YOURSELF for living a life where you put yourself out there. You must be pretty brave. No doubt you will be sharper, wittier, and sassier than ever before. It probably feels like you have new skin and you might even be proud to show it off.

Take that, LIFE.

SNAP!

The author in rehearsals with legendary composer
John Bucchino for *Cliburn at the Modern*.

Your True North May Change from Time to Time

Are you feeling the call of the wild?

You are about to make a grand exit and close the curtain on this chapter of your life.

But guess what that means. . .**new beginnings**.

Everyone has a different experience at graduation. Some have great jobs already lined up. Some are going to further their studies in graduate school. Some are completely bewildered! They have no idea how they are going to pay off student loans. Some are exhilarated because they will soon hear wedding bells. Others anticipate the loss of their core social group.

My advice is to breathe into what is presenting itself at the time. If the only thing you can think about right now is knowing where you will move all your things, or a cool interview you have coming up, or that someone has asked you to sublet their space for the summer—that's OK. Put on your mule blinders, and DO NOT COMPARE your journey to others'.

Yours is going to be the BEST one because it is YOURS.

Also, very importantly,

IT'S OKAY IF YOU
CHANGE DIRECTIONS MIDCOURSE.

Today's world might prefer that you stick with a project and see it through to the end. I find this mindset to be the number one challenge with a lot of students I teach. I definitely think it is a generational concept, and it reflects the socioeconomic time you were born in. There are a lot of distractions out there. Back to the title of this chapter. Think about what is going to matter to YOU the most in 10 or 20 years:

- That you are well-traveled?

- That you amassed enough cash to feel secure?

- That you followed your creative muse to its highest degree?

- That you focused on family?

All of these are valid.

Here's an exercise I call ***Clear Intentions.***

Write down your top three life goals at this time. Then, under each goal, explore what you want to feel as a result of having accomplished it. For example, if I devote myself to being well-traveled, how is that going to make me feel? Fulfilled, inspired, or connected? If I have a big, fat bank account and own multiple organic fast food chains (hmm—not a bad idea—feel free to borrow this one), what will I feel? Secure, stable, powerful? Only you can answer what meaning these accomplishments will bring. My suggestion is to always focus on HOW your accomplishments WILL MAKE YOU FEEL.

Opportunities both big and small will come along that may not LOOK LIKE what you imagined. I've been there, oh-so-many times, and often have been pleasantly surprised.

The reasons I'm stressing this point is because the performing arts come with a load of ego, by nature. This is normal. I have one. WE all do. Your ego can trick you into thinking this is what I *should* be doing. Ego can strike both ways. It can make you bring your very best game to a situation, or it can distort your perception of why you are aiming for a certain outcome. Here's how I imagine the world looks from the ego's point of view.

> **Your true self**: Hi Ego. My friend in NYC just told me there's a sure chance that I could get this role in an off-Broadway show as long as I can get up there this weekend to audition.
>
> **Ego**: Oh really? NYC? I am there!
>
> **True Self**: Yeah, it sounds cool, but the show is in January and only pays $100 a week.
>
> **Ego**: Who cares? It's FRIGGIN' NYC!!
>
> **True Self**: Yes, I know. It would be amazing for my resume to do something that's on the East Coast.

Ego: Right; stay with that. It's the only way I'm gonna be happy.

True Self: Well, settle down. I want to do it, but I just got a call to be the director for this community theater. It pays $500 a week, and they put me up for free in a spa house with servants (OK, this is a stretch).

Ego: Talk to the hand. No way. New York is better. I've been told it is the crème de la crème. "You ain't nuttin' if you ain't New Yawk, baby!"

True Self: Yes, deep down, I've always wanted to be up there.

Ego: Yes, and no one is gonna care or notice you if you take the job in that Podunk theater.

True Self: Well, I dunno. The Artistic Director told me I can apply for some grants and possibly take this show for a showcase in NYC next spring with the right cast.

Ego: Still not big enough. I thought you wanted to feel important????

Okay, you see where I am going. By definition, New York is played up as the proof of MAKING IT, and, for many, IT IS. There's no right or wrong here. I am merely suggesting that when you broaden your definition of achievement and compare opportunities to your list of "What I Want to Feel," you start noticing options that you may not have considered, that are actually rather pleasant.

The happy ending to the story is that True Self went to the audition for the experience and to check things out. Even though True Self was offered the job in NYC, True Self ended up taking the director's job instead. After a successful run, True Self was able to apply for funding to take the show to an off-Broadway venue in NYC and ended up hiring performers that True Self had previously met at the NYC audition. It all led to multiple opportunities to collaborate with other New York theaters and artsy types.

Word of Advice: Keep a compass but don't freak out if North changes a bit now and then. Just think of a GPS voice saying, "REROUTING. REROUTING."

Guys and Dolls at my alma mater HSU
with Gary Stroope as Sky Masterson.

Let's Play a Game

I'd like to invite you to play a little game. It could help you know that your higher self is always there for you—giving you support even in the most daunting times. Games, visioning, and playfulness are the mind's way of getting out of the rut. The creative mind sends messages to us in metaphor/symbols and sometimes in surprising ways.

So here we go...

I am going to describe five images I would like you to consider. The legend or key to your answers will be at the bottom.

PLEASE DON'T READ the legend until you are finished doing all the exercises. You will spoil all the fun and perhaps miss an opportunity for an awe-inspiring moment. I encourage you to approach these questions with a sense of wonder and open mindedness. Think about how you would like to feel guided about your next right step to fulfillment.

Let's play!

~ Take a deep breath

~ Close your eyes

~ Relax

~ Let go

Go with your first impression. Don't overthink the questions. Write down your answers.

See in your mind's eye a scene as if it were a movie. There is conflict, uncertainty. Describe the character. What is happening?

1. Imagine that you are hearing a song that you find encouraging. Who is singing it? What are some of the lyrics? How does that song make you feel?

_____

_____

_____

_____

_____

_____

_____

_____

_____

_____

THE NEXT ACT

2. Suppose that you're enjoying an invigorating walk and you come upon a festival. There is activity on one of the large stages. Action, energy, joy. Suddenly you notice you are watching yourself on that stage. Describe what is going on? Who is there with you on the stage?

3. Visualize a scene where something strong and lasting is being built. What are the different tools and machines that are being used?

4. Envision that you are sitting on a beach—you feel relaxed and happy. There's no-one else on the beach. The temperature is just right and the sun is starting to set. Gradually you look out and see something gently floating from the sky. A pleasant sight of an object, as if being handed down from heavens. It makes you feel happy or strong. What is this object?

_____

_____

_____

_____

_____

_____

_____

_____

_____

_____

_____

_____

_____

_____

_____

_____

_____

_____

_____

_____

_____

_____

_____

Legend:

OOOPs, wait. Halt! No cheating!

Did you do the exercises? If not, get back and don't spoil your fun.

If, AND ONLY IF, you answered all the questions on the previous pages, should you proceed to the legend below. Your higher-self is trying to give you a message. Try not to be too literal. Remember your higher-self is a benevolent force that uses creativity, pictures, and feelings as its language.

Number 1 describes your current state of affairs. What is happening? Are you the hero or victim? What is the climate of the scene? How does it make you feel as you envisioned it? Are there possibilities around you? Any clues? Remember this may simply be stating what is present or what you have recently experienced.

Number 2 is an invitation for change. What are the lyrics you hear? Does the group or singer have any special meaning to you? Is the song encouraging you in a certain direction or confirming what you already thought to be true?

Number 3 is an indication of where you are headed. What you see on the stage are elements of what is possible in your world. Is there dancing, connecting, perfection, collaboration, thrills, artful moments, money raining down, colors?

Number 4 is a picture of a method of how you need to go about building this dream. What are the tools for? What do they symbolize? What is being built? A bridge? A building with many compartments? A beautiful statue for the whole town to see? What do you need to take note of?

Number 5 is a symbol that has been given to you as a picture of support. A talisman with a bit of magic and a reminder. Imagine taking that symbol with your dominant hand and bringing it into your body. What does that symbol mean to you? Your unconscious mind will always speak to you in your own symbols. What could it be implying as you go forward with your goals? Notice how that symbol shows up for you in the next few days wherever you go. Perhaps you may want to draw it in your journal or make post it notes and put them all over your home. Discuss that symbol with trusted friends.

Concert pianist Spencer Myer and the author for
Musical Awakenings.

Wellness for the Performer's Life

Bottom line: *You are an athlete.*

As an artist you must merge your psyche and emotions. This combination must translate to the audience and it happens in a fairly precarious environment. (Wow! And you thought it was just about singing.) I say precarious because of the musty old theaters with large over-hanging equipment, curtains, and clunky stage pieces. You do half of your movement in the dark or low light. Huge set pieces are moved in the black. Generally you are working with an ensemble, which increases your exposure to germs and the latest malady. Wigs, costumes, and quick changes make you sweat. Non-professional theater spaces are often not regulated, nor cleaned. I can't tell you how many times I have brought my own cloth to ensure the piano was dusted prior to a performance. Constant heavy makeup can be torture for sensitive skin.

But why do we do it? Because we love it!!! There's no business like show business. There is no exhilaration quite like it. So, to keep the joy in the journey here are a few tips. If I sound like a hypochondriac just remember classical singers have what are called our "money notes." These extremely high or low notes sit right on the comfortable edge of our vocal range. It's these notes that raise the hair on the back of an audience's necks and makes them want to jump up in great applause. Consider the ballerina who must do 20 pirouettes across the stage, flawlessly, night after night, even though her one ankle is slightly sprained. There is a lot of pressure on a performer to bring his "A" game, regardless of personal concern.

Most people continue to perform because they just have to. It is an inner drive. Performing heightens the senses and creates a variety of intimate experiences with fellow performers and with your audience.

You cannot underestimate your physical needs and the significance of the quality of the environment in which you work if you desire a long term career in the arts.

In short: *You are your environment.*

Any investment in protecting or improving your health, whether it is food, sleep, massages, or exercise is a wise choice, and frankly, not wasted. Taking care of *you* is a savvy choice for stardom. Adjusting to your body's needs is paramount if you travel often. Always be cognizant of the necessary recovery time needed after a big project. It's not just about the body; it's also about taking care of your "sensitivities" and realizing the amount of energy you have used. Be quietly mindful about all you have been a part of, and prioritize doing what's right for you. I was always known as the one who skipped the parties after performances when there were still five shows to carry out. I simply couldn't do it all. I do however, have another great friend who says the only reason she is a performer is so she can party! Ha Ha. Each to their own. (To her credit—she did have a maid who would clean up after her glorious gatherings.)

You need to consider the long haul as a performer. Sustainability, if you will.

Taking care of your body can help you avoid damage, injury, and other set-backs. Oh, and a small tip—frequent flying is difficult for the thyroid, which, in turn, affects your energy. The need for enough water is emphasized so much these days and should not be underestimated especially for singers.

Here is a list of guidelines to follow if you become ill and have a sore throat or hoarseness.

1. Drink plenty of water. The late Dr. Van Lawrence, ENT for many celebrity singers at Houston Opera, as a rule, always said, "Pee pale".

2. Avoid tea, coffee, and alcohol before singing, as these can have a dehydrating effect. For proper hydration for the vocal cords you need to start the water flowing at least two hours prior to performance. This is scientifically proven by many Science of Singing Experts.

3. Take Vitamin C tablets or eat fruits/vegetables rich in Vitamin C to aid your body's natural defenses. Hot lemon & honey or blackcurrant both contain Vitamin C and antiviral properties. Fresh ginger has

natural anti-inflammatory properties—grate a little ginger and add it to hot water, sweeten with honey.

4. REST!! This includes vocal rest and remember whispering is actually taxing on the cords.

5. Severe, violent coughing can injure the vocal folds. Cough syrup and lozenges can help. Slippery elm is also a wonderful moisturizer. Sleep sitting up or propped up. This will greatly reduce your need to cough during the night. Again, coughing is a performer's nightmare.

6. Hot water steam inhalation, with or without a few drops of eucalyptus, peppermint, or other essential oil helps clear the sinuses.

7. If you can, restrict singing or speaking as much as possible, to allow the medicine to work.

8. On recovery, start with some gentle humming for 5-10 minutes at a time and slowly build up to a few vocal exercises in your mid-range, gradually expanding the range over several days. The rate of recovery will depend on the severity of illness and how experienced a singer you are. Upon a recurrence of hoarseness, stop and rest the voice for another couple of days.

9. If you consistently have mucus in the voice:

    a. Have your thyroid checked

b. Certain medications can cause more mucus production, such as blood pressure medication.

c. Consider eliminating dairy or wheat products from your diet. This can be a major game changer.

d. Mix ¼ teaspoon of apple cider vinegar with one cup of warm water. You can drink this as a tea or just gargle with it. Vinegar helps to restore alkalinity and will break up the mucus.

10. If you have chronic hoarseness, you may need a bit of speech therapy to change your approach to how you use the voice. Always have a doctor check your vocal cords if you have consistent problems. You would be amazed how your daily voice use can affect the health of the singing voice.

Here are some of my favorite "go to" methodologies for relieving stress, aligning the body, and improving breathing:

❖ Feldenkrais Method

❖ Alexander Technique

❖ Yoga

❖ Tai Chi

❖ Pilates

❖ Visualization & Affirmations

❖ Meditation

❖ Journaling

❖ SLEEP (sorry, but it needs to be said. . .)

❖ Color Therapy

❖ Acupuncture

❖ Chiropractic

❖ Reiki

❖ Foot Reflexology

Wow, I could write a whole book on these topics. If a certain treatment interests you, check it out. Also, get referrals from friends.

Regarding Travel:

Never leave home without *peppermint oil* in your pocket. It will relieve a thousand ailments. When mixed with warm water and gargled, it refreshes breath and lessens a cough. Mixed with water, a few sips can settle your stomach. And if a child in seat 4B suddenly chucks the yogurt he shouldn't have eaten, you can sprinkle it on a tissue to abate the stench. OH YES! This happened to me on a small prop plane, where we sat knees-to-noses. I KNEW I couldn't bear the smell of ripe yogurt, so I sprinkled some drops on my tissue, waved it around, and began to breathe vigorously while I averted my gaze. And last but not least, if you feel nauseated or get a headache, sprinkle a few drops on a cool, wet cloth and hold it on the back of your neck—it will do wonders.

Don't be shy about bringing a cool-mist humidifier with you for your hotel room, especially in arid climates. It is a shock to sing in Colorado or New Mexico. You'll discover how difficult it is to get a good, deep breath or keep moisture in your throat. I have small travel versions of humidifiers to keep in my suitcase—COMPLETE LIFESAVERS.

Get regular blood tests and physicals. Treat your body well. It's the only one you have! And if you are a woman, you might be thinking of making other little performers someday, your biggest creative project ever, so you want to take care of yourself. Our bodies are divine, but we often drag them along to do our bidding. Eventually the body wins, so make friends with it. Let your body be your best ally and she will serve you for a lifetime.

I love to have fun with my pianists.
This is Adam Stout backstage at Songbird Live!

Stay Gracious Always without Expectations

Have you heard the phrase *"grace under fire?"*

In the performing world, it is usually required. Here, I'm speaking of the moments that make you sweat and the people who can push your buttons. You have auditions, long rehearsals, exhilarating opening nights, travel woes, rejections, and even exciting opportunities to be the understudy. Even luckier, you might have a chance to be featured in the media! You go through competitions, rude choreographers who can't count, and emotionally distant casting directors who won't give you a clue or any feedback as to why they never hired you. Oh, and did I mention paying your bills while looking like you haven't been struggling through those eight shows per week? There is value in the question, **"Is there anything else you like to do?"**

There are varied opportunities to express one's art without doing it as a profession. However, I do trust the artist's gut instinct. Sometimes there is a quiet knowing, a yearning to perform. When asked what is it you want to do my reply was always, *"I just know I have to sing."* It WAS the one thing I knew for sure. Even though I didn't have any other answers. But after taking a pedagogy class, I discovered that I loved teaching as well.

But let's get back to the point. Why emphasize graciousness?

First, what is graciousness?

> Webster's definition: *Marked by kindness, tact, and courtesy.*

> My definition: *Graciousness is the ability to think in a larger and more inclusive way.*

Graciousness is perceiving, at a higher level, that there is enough for everyone and that serving others will, in some way, come back to serve you. For example, if you are in an ensemble with someone, it helps the whole team if you check on others, give them the stage, and point out their accomplishments. And most importantly, THESE PEOPLE WILL CIRCLE BACK IN YOUR LIFE!!

Challenging work relationships are unavoidable. I have found the most petty environments tended to be the chorus in musical theater. I am not sure why. Maybe it was because of the very few jobs that existed. It was often downright nasty, and nerves would get frayed. The best advice I can give is:

> *Try not to be a doormat, shine when it's your moment, and use the best mule blinders you can.*

Focus on the job at hand and acknowledge others as often as you can. It is a prickly environment and sometimes cannot be avoided. Humor will help. Getting others to laugh with you is a relief for everyone.

Secondly, dance with the one that "brung" you.

If someone has had the wherewithal to help you get a gig, hire you, or speak up for you, then, by all means, regard them whenever you can. A person who opens doors for you is your most valuable asset. Hopefully, in the future, you can pay it forward and do the same for other artists.

The most endearing thing you can do for your career is to collaborate, feature other people, and give them a chance to shine. That light reflects back on you and believe me, will warm you on cold nights.

§§§

Light gives of itself freely, filling all available space. It does not seek anything in return; it asks not whether you are friend or foe. It gives of itself and is not thereby diminished.

~Michael Strassfeld

The enigmatic Buddy Bray on New Year's before Van Cliburn took the stage. Me? I led the audience in a conga line!

Diva's Rockin' Resources

Here is a small list of resources that are super creative and handy. Learn from the experts, I say. Why not have fun doing so?

Self-Awareness Assessment Tools

I learned about this **Character Strengths Assessment Tool** from a friend who was taking an online course for Positivity at Harvard University. This assessment has inspired many "ah-ha" moments for my friends and students. I like it because it covers more than talents and leadership skills. More so, it helps you understand your true value system (e.g., your need to be of service, the need for beauty, etc.) and what true satisfaction might be beyond the career life. There is a free portion that is very useful. Taking this test helped a very talented modern dance student realize she wanted to focus her graduate work on dance therapy as opposed to professional dancing. See: viacharacter.org

Money, Money, Money

Lauren Bowling has created some hilarious and truthful YouTube videos about performers and finances. Lauren speaks from experience about her own struggles to repay debt and make her best life. I love her light and candid approach. Currently, she is an active consultant, author, and contributor to Huffington Post, Redbook, Women's Day, and many more publications. Check out her early YouTube posts as **L Bee and the Money Tree** in **Awkward Money Chats**. I enjoy watching them and she has sound advice for people who have stretched themselves financially thin, either through college debt or other career investments. She even has advice for the millennials on how to buy a home! Connect with her newest brand: financialbestlife.com.

Vocal/Speech Therapy Assistance

Kristie Knickerbocker, owner and speech therapist at the **A Tempo Voice Center** in Texas, created some wonderful tools, ideas, and games to assist you with vocal health. Speech therapy can be an important key if you are experiencing vocal distress or constant hoarseness. I find her tools to be engaging and playful. Her website is: atempovoicecenter.com

To find a qualified speech therapist in your area, see: pava-vocology.org

Dealing with Anxiety

Rudy Hunter has the coolest meditations and "woo woo" recordings for you and your pet. Rudy was a dancer in NYC until he broke his back. He has an amazing story and now leads people to accept healing energy. He understands the performer's life. He has an entire page devoted to free offerings for help with grieving, anxiety, PTSD (especially helpful for Veterans)—and so any more. His approach is simple and uncluttered. Find him at rudyhunter.com.

Business Cards, Flyers, Cover Designs, and other Illustrations

Jae Lin, of DoodleMeAlive, is a talented artist with many wonderful ideas! Graphic design, typography, and illustrations are her specialty. Friendly and lovingly crafted logos, posters, web icons and assets, and more!

Find her portfolio at: behance.net/doodlemealive
Contact her at: doodlemealive@gmail.com

Now just a bear chasing a honey bee,
at DFW Open Mic Classical.

A Better Version of Yourself

I want to leave you with the most important advice I can give you for anything:

You are love. It's all love. Allow love.

The reason we seek to excel is because, deep down, there is something we love about ourselves. We may not recognize it as love. It could be covered over with fear and doubt. For sure, I know we are seeking love, and therefore, craving experiences in the world that will provide a sense of purpose and belonging. When you come to see that you have a talent in you that needs to be nurtured, this is your very first child, in a sense. Your talents, whatever form they may take, are the God-Spark, a brilliant point of creation that is so uniquely **you.**

I wish I could prevent things from happening in your life that might bring disappointment or pain. But that would also mean preventing the extreme highs that happen along the way.

MY CHALLENGE TO YOU: Consider everything that happens from this point forward as all love. I am not suggesting that you stay in jobs or relationships that undermine your spirit or make your life too much of a burden. I would, however, invite you to consider that you are already enough. Embrace this simple philosophy. Allow uncertainty to be a clue. Allow the uncertainty to inform you. Your inner voice may be telling you, *"I need to practice this one more time. I need more information. I need to workshop this first."*

Hone your talent and live out that passion. Remember, every casting director, significant other, boss, and choreographer are all trying to do the same thing as you— prove that they are someone in this world. Not all will be equipped to communicate that in the healthiest ways. If you can remember this, you might be able to observe their sometimes harsh actions or judgment through the eyes of understanding. Then, you will know that their response is not a reflection of your ability or worth. Sometimes it's best to move on, find a new herd, shake off what didn't work, and seek higher ground.

I wish you success in all your endeavors. Remember I had fun teaching you. You were important to me. Carry on the tradition of making hot tea for all those you love. More than anything, I wish you the courage to be all *you.*

Your talent can, at times, feel like it is buried beneath a hugely crusted over chunk of dirt. Beneath it is your talent, a small trickle of water, an imperceptible stream, which is winding its way in the desert, seeking its own level. Sometimes, you can only be the water, the trickle, waiting for a gust of wind to blow away the residue above you.

Remember water dissolves the stone with time and persistence. Plus you don't have to be better than all the other streamlets around you. All the water is needed. We need your unique fluidity and refreshment. Here is the last line of the syllabus from a course I teach.

"I don't expect you to be as good as someone else in this class. We all have our strengths. I hope to encourage you however—to be a better version of yourself than you thought possible."

§§§

A thousand days of heat, withers the rose
But one drop of rain can make it live again.

~ Colleen Hughes Mallette

The author and Keith Critcher amuse often with "Lime Jello Marshmellow Cottage Cheese Surprise" by William Bolcomb. Even the Scots liked it at the Edinburgh Fringe Festival 2000. Best travel bud.

Clarity through Inquiry Worksheets

~ Exercise 1 ~

Instructions: Please don't think too hard on these. Each exercise is meant to stimulate some new ideas. You might discuss them with a friend, or scribble and draw in the space provided. Try to suspend judgment.

1. The 3 biggest things impacting my life right now are:

Thing One:

_____

_____

_____

_____

_____

_____

_____

_____

_____

Thing Two:

_____
_____
_____
_____
_____
_____
_____
_____
_____
_____
_____
_____

Thing Three:

_____
_____
_____
_____
_____
_____
_____
_____
_____
_____
_____
_____

2. On a scale of 1-10 (10 being the highest), my stress is about Level: _____.

3. Some situations that are NOT working for me right now are:

_____

_____

_____

_____

_____

_____

_____

_____

_____

_____

_____

_____

_____

_____

_____

_____

_____

_____

_____

_____

_____

_____

_____

_____

_____

_____

4. If finances weren't a concern, I would consider these as options for the upcoming year, (e.g., backpack abroad, take a job that I consider temporary, hit the local audition scene). Describe, in detail, what a typical day might be:

5. These are some steps I can take to make one of these options happen (make a list):

6. Make a list of some tentative deadlines needed to accomplish the above list. (Remember just making a phone call or doing internet research is a step.):

7. Possible reasons I am not moving forward:

·Fear of not being good enough.

·I have received feedback that I need more training.

·It's not what my family wants me to do.

·I have a relationship that is heavy on my mind.

·I have some health issues or other practical things that need attention first.

·I am easily distracted and need accountability.

·Perhaps my goal isn't exciting enough to get me motivated.

·Fear of getting what I want.

·Feels more like work than it does fulfillment.

·Saying yes too often to other people's agenda.

Do any of these reasons pertain to you?

_____

_____

_____

_____

_____

_____

_____

_____

_____

8. I need to do the following things, THIS WEEK, to help me gain more clarity, (e.g., clean out a closet, deal with taxes, sign up for auditions, redo resume, get head shots, go to the gym, meditate):

~ Exercise 2 ~

1. Besides my obvious talents, these are things I seem to do really well. Nothing is too simple, (e.g., organize spaces, lift people up, keep focused, repair things):

_____

_____

_____

_____

_____

_____

_____

_____

_____

2. List as many things as you can that you have done well, gotten through, or completed in the past two years. Don't hold back. List things as mundane as "went to new auditions", "learned scripts", etc.:

_____

_____

_____

_____

_____

_____

_____

_____

_____

_____

_____

_____

_____

_____

_____

_____

_____

_____

_____

_____

_____

_____

3.Random hobbies I love:

_____

_____

_____

_____

_____

_____

_____

_____

_____

_____

_____

_____

_____

_____

_____

_____
_____
_____
_____
_____
_____
_____
_____
_____
_____
_____

4. Describe here, in detail, a good day at work that you love:

_____
_____
_____
_____
_____
_____
_____
_____
_____
_____
_____
_____
_____
_____
_____
_____

_____
_____
_____
_____
_____
_____
_____
_____
_____
_____
_____
_____

5. If you were to ask for help to accomplish your goals, what kind of help would you ask for?

_____
_____
_____
_____
_____
_____
_____
_____
_____
_____
_____
_____
_____
_____

6. Who are 10 people, right now, that you might ask for feedback, encouragement, or advice?

(Remember: It might be beneficial to find a therapist, spiritual director, or coach to help guide you. It's smart to have a brief interview to see if you two are a good fit. We limit many good opportunities because we don't really have enough information. Doesn't hurt to shop around.)

1._____

2._____

3._____

4._____

5._____

6. _____

7. _____

8. _____

9. _____

10. _____

7. Motivation makes all the difference when reaching for a goal. Which of the following statements might be true for you? Circle 3.

· A need to be of service.

· A need to belong to a community.

· A need to have fun.

· A need to express my talent.

· A need for financial security.

· A need to start a family.

· A need to explore and be free.

· A need to discipline my life.

· A need for fame.

· A need to be respected.

·A need to achieve.

·A need to be at peace.

·A need for balance.

·A need to create a group experience.

·A need to create a legacy.

·Other.

8. Can you describe some of the road blocks that you have encountered recently which have obstructed you from achieving some of your goals?

THE NEXT ACT

~ Exercise 3 ~

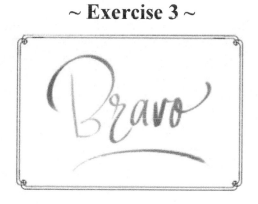

Use this chart to notice what may be influencing your mind set.

1 means: Needs improvement. **10 means:** Doing great!

Exercise, Movement:
1   2   3   4   5   6   7   8   9   10

Diet:
1   2   3   4   5   6   7   8   9   10

Sleep:
1   2   3   4   5   6   7   8   9   10

Stimulants (caffeine, power drinks, chemical):
1   2   3   4   5   6   7   8   9   10

Time in Nature:
1   2   3   4   5   6   7   8   9   10

Socializing:
1   2   3   4   5   6   7   8   9   10

Distractions (shopping, gambling, movies, video games, drugs, alcohol):
1   2   3   4   5   6   7   8   9   10

Digital and Electronic World (cell phones, computers, tablets, television, etc.):
1   2   3   4   5   6   7   8   9   10

Health Concerns:
1   2   3   4   5   6   7   8   9   10

Goal Setting:
1   2   3   4   5   6   7   8   9   10

Touch/Affection:
1   2   3   4   5   6   7   8   9   10

Playfulness/Laughter:
1   2   3   4   5   6   7   8   9   10

SCORING:

If you scored **105-130**:
It appears that you are in a great zone - in fact, keep moving right along.
If you scored **65-104**:
Try to boost a few points here and there. Notice what feels better.
If you scored **13-65**:
This is a REALLY challenging time. Try to bring at least one area up a few points, and you will notice the difference in your mood. I promise - you are not alone.

Make a fun poster or buy a new journal to chart your progress. Funny pictures, stickers, colored pens - why not enjoy?? Many students report tangible progress from making a Vision Board.

~ Exercise 4 ~

These statements are geared toward the performing arts but can also be utilized for other professional aspirations, (e.g., instead of "My dream roles" substitute "My dream position."):

1. My dream roles to play are:

2. My top three performances, to date, have been:

i:

_____

_____

_____

ii:

_____

_____

_____

iii:

_____

_____

_____

3. This is what I would like to read in a review about my performance:

4. For me, it would be great to be paid _____ for my future performances.

5. Put in order how you would prioritize:

MONEY

FREEDOM

FAME

PERSONAL SATISFACTION

ADVENTURE

INFLUENCE ON OTHERS

6. These are people I admire for their accomplishments:

_____

_____

_____

_____

_____

_____

_____

_____

_____

_____

_____

_____

_____

_____

_____

_____

_____

_____

_____

_____

_____

_____

_____

_____

_____

_____

7. If I raised the bar 20% on what I thought was possible, I might try what?

8. True or False?

I am most happy as a solo performer: _____.

I am most happy in an ensemble: _____.

9. Yes or No:

I would like to recreate a standard:

I would like to recreate a classic:

I would prefer to do more original work:

10. If I need to have a second job to make money as I work toward my desires, I am considering:

_____

_____

_____

_____

_____

_____

_____

_____

_____

_____

_____

_____

Afterword

Three years have passed since I began compiling this handbook. Today is October 6, 2017.

The past twelve months have been extraordinarily tumultuous for, really, everyone in the world; *wars, senseless cruelty, secrets, chaos, horrific natural disasters.* The anxiety and uncertainty is palpable. My heart especially goes out to young creative types who haven't quite etched out their way in the world. Since August 21st, 2017 current events have escalated.

Interesting. That was the day of a huge solar eclipse.

If you have stumbled upon a copy of this guidebook many years from now, then, *wow*, you made it. There is a futuristic part of me that would love to think you found this guidebook in an attic or a magic tunnel. That you blew off the dust and sat down to read a few pages. Although it is not like me to be apocalyptic, I do feel a responsibility to acknowledge what is true. **Chaos is always part of great creativity.** Destruction is how the new comes forth. We must cut the cloth to make the dress. Volcanoes wreak havoc—then new growth comes from the fertile ash. You end a relationship and are hurled toward the one that really works. I really believe we are entering a new phase of better living, however slow it may appear.

Engage with the Author

For further booking info regarding:

~ The Next Act Workshops
~ Master Classes
~ Concerts
~ Consultations
~ Creativity Retreats
~ Along with Ms. Mallette's Comedy Delights

Contact:
Email: TheNextAct.colleen@gmail.com

Website: highcdiva.tumblr.com

Join me on Facebook: Colleen Mallette—The High C Diva
Performances and Public Appearances

Made in the USA
Coppell, TX
16 July 2021

59045745R00062